Native Americans Make History

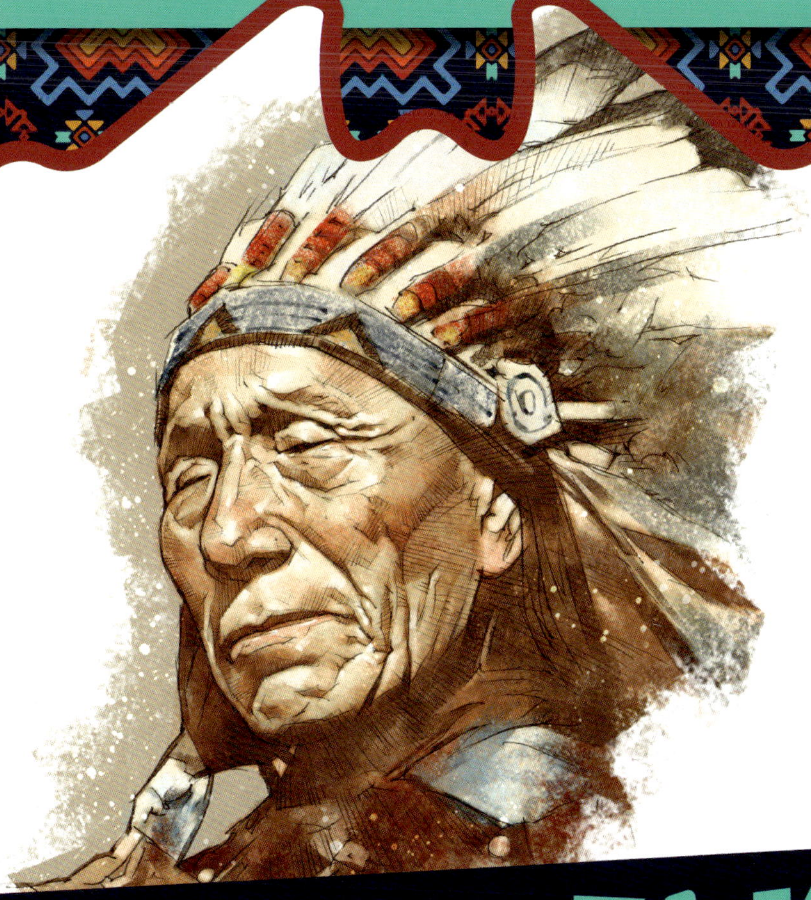

BLACK ELK

Enslow PUBLISHING

INVESTIGATE!

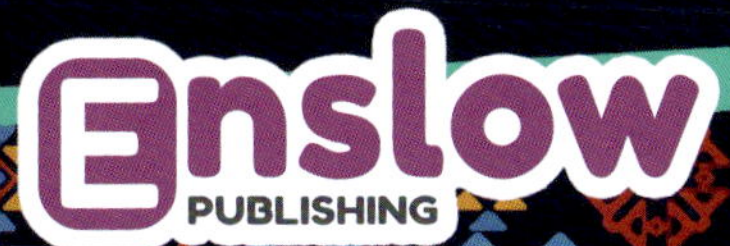

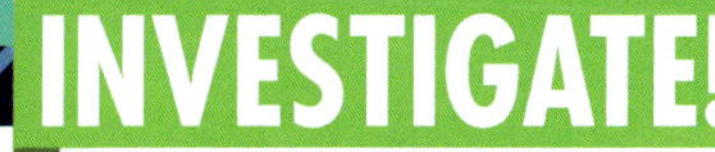

Abby Badach Doyle

Please visit our website, www.enslow.com. For a free color catalog of all our high-quality books, call toll free 1-800-398-2504 or fax 1-877-980-4454.

Library of Congress Cataloging-in-Publication Data
Names: Doyle, Abby Badach, author.
Title: Black Elk / Abby Badach Doyle.
Description: New York : Enslow Publishing, [2023] | Series: Native Americans make history | Includes bibliographical references and index.
Identifiers: LCCN 2021050327 (print) | LCCN 2021050328 (ebook) | ISBN 9781978527560 (library binding) | ISBN 9781978527546 (paperback) | ISBN 9781978527553 (set) | ISBN 9781978527577 (ebook)
Subjects: LCSH: Black Elk, 1863-1950–Juvenile literature. | Oglala Indians–Biography–Juvenile literature. | Oglala Indians–Religion–Juvenile literature.
Classification: LCC E99.O3 D689 2023 (print) | LCC E99.O3 (ebook) | DDC 978.004/9752440092 [B]–dc23/eng/20211116
LC record available at https://lccn.loc.gov/2021050327
LC ebook record available at https://lccn.loc.gov/2021050328

Portions of this work were originally authored by Miriam Coleman and published as *The Life of Black Elk*. All new material in this edition authored by Abby Badach Doyle.

Published in 2023 by
Enslow Publishing
29 E. 21st Street
New York, NY 10010

Designer: Leslie Taylor
Editor: Abby Badach Doyle

Photo credits: cover image Sarawut Itsaranuwut/Shutterstock.com; series background (cover and interior, Native American pattern) Dmitriy NDM/Shutterstock.com; series artwork Nevada31/Shutterstock.com; p. 5 (Black Elk photo) Walter Bernard Hunt/Marquette University Archives; p. 5 Pshenichka/Shutterstock.com; p. 5 outerbounding/Shutterstock.com; p. 7 Catmando/Shutterstock.com; p. 9 (dream image) Jozef Klopacka/Shutterstock.com; p. 9 (medicine hoop) LeondeZ/Shutterstock.com; p. 11 (painting) Everett Collection/Shutterstock.com; p. 11 (monument) Don Mammoser/Shutterstock.com; p. 11 (Custer photo) courtesy of the Library of Congress; p. 13 (bison) Green Mountain Exposure/Shutterstock.com; p. 13 (map) https://en.wikipedia.org/wiki/File:Siouxreservationmap.png; p. 15 (horse dancer) Aaron Rutten/Shutterstock.com; p. 15 (tipi cover) The Metropolitan Museum of Art; p. 17 (Black Hills) https://commons.wikimedia.org/wiki/File:Black_Elk_Wilderness_South_Dakota_5.jpg; p. 17 (bird, butterflies) toriru/Shutterstock.com; p. 17 (reservation photo) https://commons.wikimedia.org/wiki/File:Salesman_and_Indian_with_model_house_built_to_scale_on_the_back_of_a_truck._Town_of_Oglala._-_NA%E2%80%A6; p. 19 (Buffalo Bill Cody) https://commons.wikimedia.org/wiki/File:Buffalo_Bill_Cody_by_Burke,_1892.jpg; p. 19 (poster) Copyright by Courier Litho. Co., Buffalo, N.Y./LOC.com; p. 21 (Queen Victoria) https://commons.wikimedia.org/wiki/File:1887_postcard_of_Queen_Victoria.jpg; p. 21 https://commons.wikimedia.org/wiki/File:Black_Elk_and_Elk_of_the_Oglala_Lakota_-1887.jpg; pp. 23 (inset), 25 (cannons) Everett Collection/Alamy.com; p. 23 courtesy of the Library of Congress; p. 25 (top) https://commons.wikimedia.org/wiki/File:Woundedkneeencampment.jpg; p. 25 (engraving) https://commons.wikimedia.org/wiki/File:The_opening_of_the_fight_at_Wounded_Knee_by_Frederic_Remington_1891.jpg; p. 27 (family) https://commons.wikimedia.org/wiki/File:Black_Elk.jpg; p. 27 (church) http://www.marquette.edu/library/collections/archives/copyright.html; p. 28 https://en.wikipedia.org/wiki/File:Black_Elk_Speaks.jpg; p. 29 (Ben Black Elk) http://www.marquette.edu/library/archives/general.shtml; p. 29 (at gravesite) http://www.marquette.edu/library/collections/archives/copyright.html.

Printed in the United States of America

CPSIA compliance information: Batch #CSENS23: For further information contact Enslow Publishing, New York, New York, at 1-800-398-2504.

CONTENTS

Words in the glossary appear in **bold** type the first time they are used in the text.

A GREAT HEALER

In the late 1800s, the United States was expanding, or spreading, west. White American settlers moved to the Great Plains to build homes or mine for gold. However, this was a dark time in history for Native Americans. Settlers forced them to leave their homes and land. The U.S. government made it illegal to practice Native American **rituals** in public, like dances.

Black Elk lived through many important Native American battles and events. He was a wise man and a strong leader. He kept his tribe's **culture** alive during a time of great change.

tools used to mix plants

Black Elk Peak, South Dakota

Black Elk spent his life educating others about Native American beliefs.

Explore More!

Black Elk was known as a medicine man. Native Americans believe a medicine man is someone who has special powers. They say a medicine man can heal people using objects found in nature. Women can hold this position too.

EARLY YEARS

Black Elk was born in December 1863 on the Little Powder River in modern-day Wyoming. In the Lakota way of keeping time, that year was called "The Winter When Four Crows Were Killed." His family was Oglala, part of the Lakota tribe within the Great Sioux Nation.

The Lakota lived a **nomadic** life in the Great Plains. They followed herds of bison to hunt. After killing bison, the Lakota would honor the creatures' lives. As a boy, Black Elk also rode horses and played war games with his friends.

The Lakota used bison for everything, including food, tools, clothing, and housing.

Explore More!

Black Elk's father, grandfather, and great-grandfather were all named Black Elk. His father was a medicine man, as was his grandfather and several uncles. As he grew older, Black Elk learned he had this special gift too.

A POWERFUL DREAM

When Black Elk was nine years old, he got very sick. Lying ill, he had a **vision** that changed his life. In it, six grandfathers shared special knowledge of the spirit world. They gave him gifts to share their power with him. He went to a high mountain and saw a sacred hoop, or circle. He saw how the circle connected all living things.

When he awoke, Black Elk got well. His life would never be the same. He knew he had a duty to heal people and bring them together.

The sacred hoop often uses the colors black, red, yellow, and white.

Explore More!

The sacred hoop is a popular sign in Native American art. "Sacred" means blessed and important. It is sometimes called the medicine wheel. The circle shows important patterns in life, such as the seasons, life stages, or features of nature.

GOLD RUSH

Black Elk grew up in the Black Hills, which are mountains sacred to the Lakota, in present-day South Dakota and Wyoming. Trouble started in 1874, when American **prospectors** found gold there. More than 800 miners rushed in. The U.S. Army came to force Lakota people away from the area. Many Native American tribes started a village to guard their land.

In 1876, the village was attacked. Thousands of Native Americans fought back to save it, and they won. This was the Battle of the Little Bighorn. Black Elk, only 12 years old, was there for this important fight.

Indian Memorial at Little Bighorn Battlefield National Monument

The Battle of the Little Bighorn, shown here in a painting, took place in modern-day Montana.

Explore More!

The Fort Laramie Treaty of 1868 is a peace agreement between the U.S. government and Lakota leaders. In it, the U.S. government promised not to let settlers into the Black Hills. However, this treaty was broken during the gold rush.

HEADING NORTH

The Native Americans won the Battle of the Little Bighorn, but the fight continued. More soldiers came. Soon, the U.S. government took the Black Hills from the Lakota people. Many Lakota agreed to move to reservations, or pieces of land set aside by the U.S. government for Native Americans to live.

Black Elk's band kept moving north to what is now Canada. They called it "Grandmother's Land." Life was easier there at first. However, Black Elk missed his homeland. He often thought of his vision and his duty to bring people together.

Over time, the Great Sioux Reservation got smaller as the U.S. government claimed more land.

Explore More!

In Canada, Black Elk's people grew hungry and tired during the long winter. He had a vision that told him where to find bison. He led his people there, where they hunted and killed eight bison. This helped them survive the cold, snowy winter.

THE HORSE DANCE

After two years up north, Black Elk's people returned home. He was 17 years old. He still had visions and felt scared. He finally told a medicine man named Black Road.

Black Road told Black Elk to **perform** his vision in front of his people. The Lakota made it a grand ritual. They painted a tepee. They decorated horses and dressed up in special clothes. Black Elk taught them the song and dance from his dream. He was no longer afraid of his power. This is when he became a medicine man.

The dance from Black Elk's vision was called the Horse Dance. The Horse Dance costume (left) and tepee decorations (above) were used for this sacred dance.

Explore More!

When Black Elk returned home, the Oglala Lakota people no longer wandered free to follow the bison. The U.S. government moved them to a smaller piece of land called the Pine Ridge Reservation. It still exists today in southwestern South Dakota.

LIFE AT PINE RIDGE

Black Elk moved to the Pine Ridge Reservation in 1881. He was sad at how unhappy his people seemed. They lived in small log houses. They were removed from the life they had always known.

By age 19, Black Elk was well known as a healer among his people. He performed many sacred Sioux rituals to make people feel better. During this time, Black Elk spent a lot of time alone in nature. He had more visions and cried in deep sadness. He asked the spirits for understanding and wisdom.

the Black Hills

model house on the Pine Ridge Reservation, 1878

Explore More!

Black Elk said he saw signs in nature when he felt close to the spirits. Sometimes, they would appear to him in thunderstorms or rain. Other times, he saw a sign through animals, such as birds or butterflies.

BUFFALO BILL'S WILD WEST SHOW

When Black Elk was about 23, he wanted to understand the white people's world so he could help his tribe. In 1886, men from Buffalo Bill's Wild West Show arrived at the reservation. They wanted Native Americans to join their famous outdoor show to perform **traditional** dances and tricks on horseback.

Black Elk saw an opportunity to understand the ways of white people. He joined the group and traveled to big cities including New York City. He performed at Madison Square Garden for several months. He was one of the group's best dancers.

"Buffalo Bill"
William F. Cody

Buffalo Bill became one of the world's most famous people by the year 1900.

Explore More!

Buffalo Bill's Wild West Show brought a taste of American **frontier** life to cities around the world. The show had live animals, including bison and elk. Cowboys performed rope tricks and staged battles. The show ran for around 30 years.

TRAVELING OVERSEAS

The show was a huge success. In March 1887, the cast took a steamship to England. The trip was unpleasant. It took two weeks, and Black Elk got seasick. Some of the show's animals died, which made Black Elk very sad. While in England, Black Elk danced for Queen Victoria, who he called "Grandmother England."

Soon, it was time to return. Black Elk got lost and missed the ship home. He joined a different Wild West show and traveled to France, Germany, and Italy. Later, he found Buffalo Bill, who helped him get home.

Queen Victoria

Black Elk wore traditional dress for the Wild West show, including otter fur and pheasant feathers.

Black Elk became very homesick while in Paris, France. He fell ill and had another vision. In it, he rode a cloud back home to the Black Hills. When he awoke, he learned he had been close to death for three days.

A NEW MOVEMENT

Black Elk returned to Pine Ridge in 1889. The Lakota people were suffering. They were hungry, sick, and bison herds they depended on were gone. For hope, many Native Americans joined the Ghost Dance movement.

Followers of this movement believed in a vision from a native leader named Wovoka. He said this special dance would renew their early way of life. Followers believed the dance would make the bison return, bring back dead **ancestors**, and make the white settlers go away. Black Elk joined in. Soon, he became a leader of the Ghost Dance.

The Ghost Dance was similar to many other Native American dances in which participants formed a circle and often held hands.

Explore More!

Black Elk went to a Ghost Dance at Wounded Knee Creek, in what is now South Dakota. The ritual had a circle, a flowering stick, and dancers with their faces painted red. This matched what Black Elk saw in his own visions.

WOUNDED KNEE

Fearing war, the U.S. Army headed to Lakota reservations to stop the Ghost Dance. In December 1890, they met a group of Miniconjou Lakota at Wounded Knee Creek and took away their guns. Then, a Lakota man began the Ghost Dance. Others joined.

One Lakota's gun went off by accident. The U.S. Army opened fire. Terrible fighting began. Many Lakota had no guns to guard themselves. The soldiers killed more than 250 Lakota. Nearly half were women and children. Black Elk was nearby when he heard the shooting. He and others rode over to help.

reenactment of the Battle of Wounded Knee

Wounded Knee is called a massacre. This means many harmless people died.

Explore More!

Fighting continued after Wounded Knee. Black Elk was wounded. Soon, the Lakota **surrendered**. In giving up, Black Elk said he felt like he let down the ancestors who gave him those special visions.

FAMILY AND FAITH

After Wounded Knee, Black Elk lived on the Pine Ridge Reservation with other Oglala Lakota. He married Katie War Bonnet in 1892. Together, they had three children. Katie followed a faith called Roman Catholicism. Black Elk thought **religion** could help him heal people too.

He became Catholic in December 1904 and took the name Nicholas. He helped the priests on the reservation. Black Elk shared his faith with other tribes in Wyoming and Nebraska. He also still believed the traditional Lakota teachings he learned as a medicine man.

Black Elk taught others about the Catholic faith at St. Paul's Mission, a church located on the Pine Ridge Reservation.

Black Elk with daughter Lucy and wife Anna, 1910

Explore More!

Black Elk's wife Katie died in 1903. He married Anna Brings White, who had two daughters, in 1905. She was also Catholic. Together, she and Black Elk had three more children. They were married until she died in 1941.

KEEPING HISTORY ALIVE

A poet named John Neihardt visited Pine Ridge in 1930. He wanted to talk to someone about Lakota history. Black Elk, now 67, told his stories in the Lakota language. His son, Benjamin Black Elk, **translated** them into English. The men felt a deep connection as they talked. Black Elk honored Neihardt with a Lakota name, Flaming Rainbow.

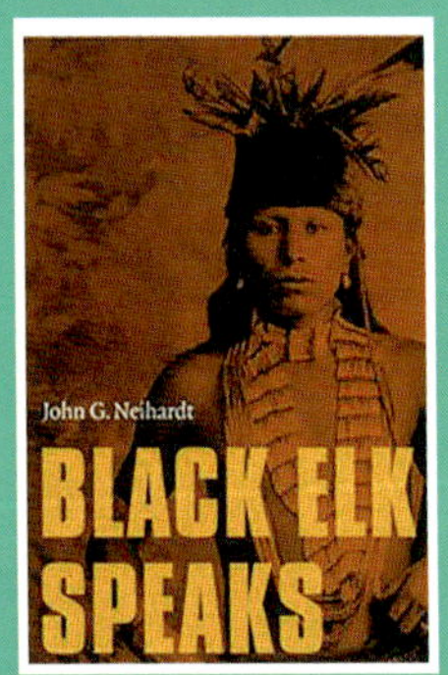

Neihardt printed his book *Black Elk Speaks* in 1932. People all over the world still read it. In August 1950, Black Elk died in South Dakota at age 86. He knew he kept Lakota culture and history alive for years to come.

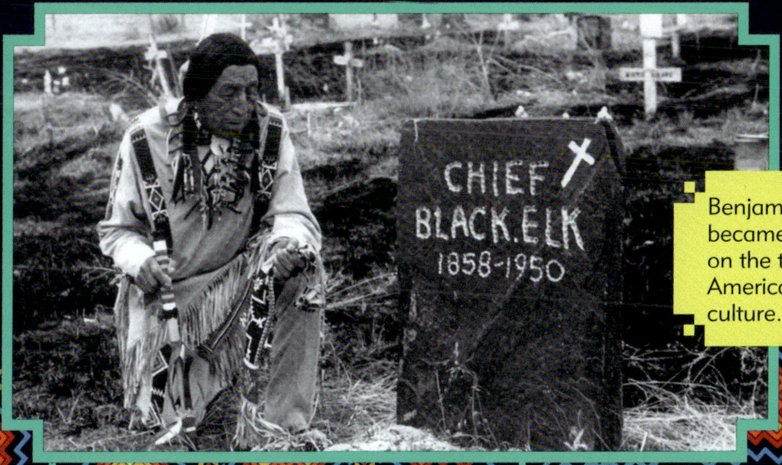

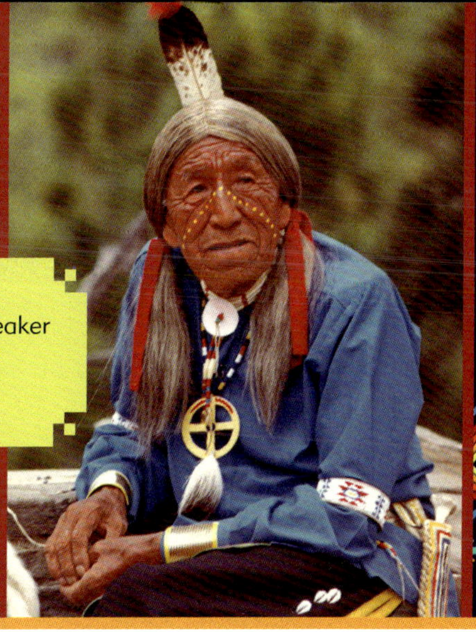

Benjamin Black Elk became a famous speaker on the topic of Native American history and culture.

THE LIFE OF BLACK ELK

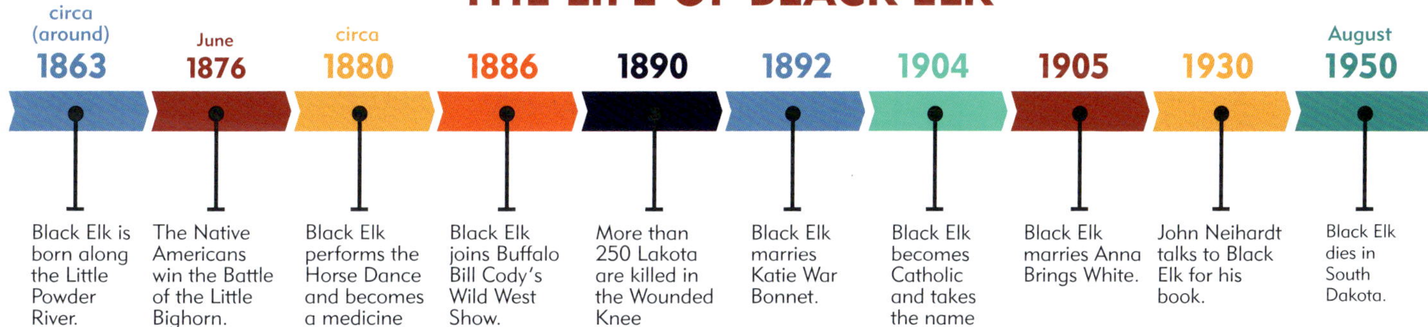

Explore More!

In 2016, U.S. leaders named the highest peak in South Dakota after Black Elk. The mountain, located in the sacred Black Hills, stands 7,242 feet (2,207.4 m) above sea level. Tribal leaders visit it every spring to honor the spirits from Black Elk's visions.

GLOSSARY

ancestor: A relative who lived long before you.

culture: The beliefs and ways of life of a group of people.

frontier: A part of a country that has been newly opened for settlement.

nomadic: Having to do with people who move from place to place.

perform: To play music or sing.

prospector: A person who searches an area for valued resources, such as gold.

religion: A belief in and way of honoring a god or gods.

ritual: A religious or formal ceremony.

surrender: To give up.

traditional: Having to do with long-practiced customs.

translate: To change words and sentences from one language into another language.

vision: Something seen by a way other than normal sight, such as in sleep or the imagination.

FOR MORE INFORMATION

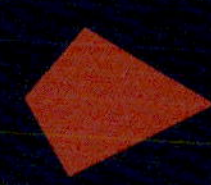

Books

Almstrom, Christine. *Grandfather Thunder and the Night Horses*. North Hampton, NH: Mindstir Media, 2017.

Nelson, S. D. *Black Elk's Vision: A Lakota Story*. New York, NY: Abrams, 2015.

Pascal, Janet B. *What Was the Wild West?* New York, NY: Grosset & Dunlap, 2017.

Websites

Lakota Language Program Resources
www.lakotalanguageproject.org/resources.html
Learn the language Black Elk spoke with an alphabet book, coloring pages, and more.

Native Americans Sioux Nation
www.ducksters.com/history/native_american_sioux_nation.php
Learn about the food, clothing, housing, and art of Black Elk's people.

Native People of the American Great Plains
www.kids.nationalgeographic.com/history/article/native-people-of-the-american-great-plains
See cool pictures and facts about the Lakota people and other Great Plains tribes.

INDEX

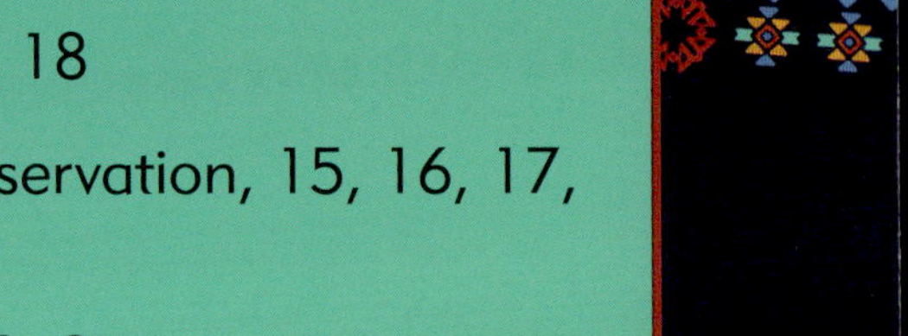